# HAPPY CROCHET!

## 13 ADORABLE PROJECTS IN BRIGHT COLORS

LEISURE ARTS, INC. • Maumelle, Arkansas

# CONTENTS

Bright Coaster Set

Wavy Cowl

Flower Mug Cozy

Oval Rug

Tasseled Pillow

Ripple Wall Hanging

# Introduction

Surround yourself with happy colors! Vivid home décor designs
that will brighten any space include a lively basket, a bold oval rug,
a set of cheery coasters and a trio of brilliant wall hangings. Toss an
exciting tasseled pillow onto your easy chair or add zest to your sofa
with a textured throw. Let your light grow with the floral touches
on the mug cozy, the notebook cover or the handy marketbag.
Perk up your wardrobe with a toasty cowl or a perfect wrap.
Find your happy place and fill it with color!

# Striped Basket

DESIGN BY MARLY BIRD

 **EASY**

**FINISHED SIZE**

10½" diameter x 11" high (at side) (26.5 cm x 28 cm)

**GAUGE**

11 hdc and 8 rows/rnds = 4" (10 cm)

**Gauge Swatch:** 5½" (14 cm) diameter Work same as Rnds 1-5 of Bottom, page 8; do **not** finish off.

Basket is worked holding two strands of yarn together throughout.

## SHOPPING LIST

**Yarn** (Medium Weight Cotton)

[2.5 ounces, 120 yards (70.9 grams, 109 meters) per ball]:

☐ Yellow - 4 balls

☐ Pink - 4 balls

☐ White - 2 balls

## Crochet Hook

☐ Size J (6 mm)

 **or** size needed for gauge

# Striped Basket

## BOTTOM

**Rnd 1** (Right side)**:** With Yellow and using an adjustable loop *(Figs. 1a-d, page 62)*, ch 2 **(does not count as a st, now and throughout)**, work 10 hdc in ring; join with slip st to top of beginning ch-2.

**Rnd 2:** Ch 2, 2 hdc in first hdc and in each hdc around; join with slip st to top of beginning ch-2: 20 hdc.

**Rnd 3:** Ch 2, hdc in first hdc, 2 hdc in next hdc, (hdc in next hdc, 2 hdc in next hdc) around; join with slip st to top of beginning ch-2: 30 hdc.

**Rnd 4:** Ch 2, hdc in first 2 hdc, 2 hdc in next hdc, (hdc in next 2 hdc, 2 hdc in next hdc) around; join with slip st to top of beginning ch-2: 40 hdc.

**Rnd 5:** Ch 2, hdc in first 3 hdc, 2 hdc in next hdc, (hdc in next 3 hdc, 2 hdc in next hdc) around; join with slip st to top of beginning ch-2: 50 hdc.

**Rnd 6:** Ch 2, hdc in first 4 hdc, 2 hdc in next hdc, (hdc in next 4 hdc, 2 hdc in next hdc) around; join with slip st to top of beginning ch-2: 60 hdc.

**Rnd 7:** Ch 2, hdc in first 5 hdc, 2 hdc in next hdc, (hdc in next 5 hdc, 2 hdc in next hdc) around; join with slip st to top of beginning ch-2: 70 hdc.

**Rnd 8:** Ch 2, hdc in first 6 hdc, 2 hdc in next hdc, (hdc in next 6 hdc, 2 hdc in next hdc) around; join with slip st to top of beginning ch-2: 80 hdc.

**Rnd 9:** Ch 2, hdc in first 7 hdc, 2 hdc in next hdc, (hdc in next 7 hdc, 2 hdc in next hdc) around; join with slip st to top of beginning ch-2: 90 hdc.

**Rnd 10:** Ch 2, hdc in first 8 hdc, 2 hdc in next hdc, (hdc in next 8 hdc, 2 hdc in next hdc) around; join with slip st to top of beginning ch-2: 100 hdc.

## SIDES

**Rnd 1:** Ch 2, working in Back Loops Only *(Fig. 3, page 62)*, sc in first hdc, dc in next hdc, (sc in next hdc, dc in next hdc) around; join with slip st to top of beginning ch-2.

**Rnds 2 and 3:** Ch 2, **turn**; working in both loops, sc in first dc, dc in next sc, (sc in next dc, dc in next sc) around; join with slip st to top of beginning ch-2.

**Rnd 4:** Ch 2, turn; sc in first dc, dc in next sc, (sc in next dc, dc in next sc) around; cut one strand of Yellow, join with slip st to top of beginning ch-2 changing to one strand of Pink and remaining strand of Yellow *(Fig. 5d, page 63)*.

**Rnd 5:** Ch 2, turn; sc in first dc, dc in next sc, (sc in next dc, dc in next sc) around; cut Yellow, join with slip st to top of beginning ch-2 changing to two strands of Pink.

**Rnds 6 and 7:** Ch 2, turn; sc in first dc, dc in next sc, (sc in next dc, dc in next sc) around; join with slip st to top of beginning ch-2.

**Rnd 8:** Ch 2, turn; sc in first dc, dc in next sc, (sc in next dc, dc in next sc) around; cut one strand of Pink, join with slip st to top of beginning ch-2 changing to one strand of White and remaining strand of Pink.

**Rnd 9:** Ch 2, turn; sc in first dc, dc in next sc, (sc in next dc, dc in next sc) around; cut Pink, join with slip st to top of beginning ch-2 changing to two strands of White.

**Rnds 10 and 11:** Ch 2, turn; sc in first dc, dc in next sc, (sc in next dc, dc in next sc) around; join with slip st to top of beginning ch-2.

**Rnd 12:** Ch 2, turn; sc in first dc, dc in next dc, (sc in next dc, dc in next dc) around; cut one strand of White, join with slip st to top of beginning ch-2 changing to one strand of Yellow and remaining strand of White.

**Rnd 13:** Ch 2, turn; sc in first dc, dc in next sc, (sc in next dc, dc in next sc) around; cut White, join with slip st to top of beginning ch-2 changing to two strands of Yellow.

**Rnds 14-16:** Ch 2, turn; sc in first dc, dc in next sc, (sc in next dc, dc in next sc) around; join with slip st to top of beginning ch-2.

**Rnd 17:** Ch 2, turn; sc in first dc, dc in next sc, (sc in next dc, dc in next sc) around; cut one strand of Yellow, join with slip st to top of beginning ch-2 changing to one strand of Pink and remaining strand of Yellow.

**Rnd 18:** Ch 2, turn; sc in first dc, dc in next sc, (sc in next dc, dc in next sc) around; cut Yellow, join with slip st to top of beginning ch-2 changing to two strands of Pink.

**Rnd 19:** Ch 2, turn; sc in first dc, dc in next sc, (sc in next dc, dc in next sc) around; join with slip st to top of beginning ch-2; do **not** finish off.

## HANDLES

**Rnd 1:** Ch 2, turn; sc in first dc, dc in next sc, (sc in next dc, dc in next sc) 7 times, ch 15, skip next 15 sts, (dc in next sc, sc in next dc) 17 times, dc in next sc, ch 15, skip next 15 sts, dc in next sc, (sc in next dc, dc in next sc) around; join with slip st to top of beginning ch-2: 70 sts and 30 chs.

**Rnd 2:** Ch 2, turn; sc in first dc, dc in next sc, (sc in next st, dc in next st) around; join with slip st to top of beginning ch-2: 100 sts.

**Rnds 3-5:** Ch 2, turn; sc in first dc, dc in next sc, (sc in next dc, dc in next sc) around; join with slip st to top of beginning ch-2.

Finish off.

# Bright Coaster Set

■■□□ **EASY**

## SHOPPING LIST

**Yarn** (Medium Weight Cotton)
[2.5 ounces, 120 yards
(70.9 grams, 109 meters) per ball]:

☐ Yellow - 25 yards (23 meters)

☐ Pink - 25 yards (23 meters)

☐ Orange - 25 yards (23 meters)

☐ Green - 25 yards (23 meters)

## Crochet Hook

☐ Size H (5 mm)

**or** size needed for gauge

## COASTER

Ch 16.

**Row 1** (Wrong side)**:** Sc in back ridge of second ch from hook and each ch across *(Fig. 2, page 62)*: 15 sc.

*Note:* Loop a short piece of yarn around the **back** of any stitch on Row 1 as **right** side.

**Row 2:** Ch 1, turn; working in Back Loops Only of sc on Row 1 **and** in one free loop of beginning ch *(Fig. A)*, sc in each st across.

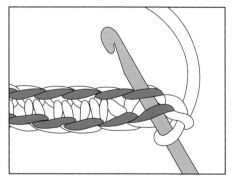

**Fig. A**

**Rows 3-22:** Ch 1, turn; working in Back Loops Only of sts on last row **and** in free loops of previous row *(Fig. B)*, sc in each st across.

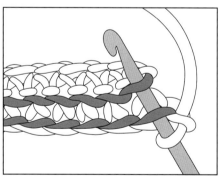

**Fig. B**

**Row 23:** Ch 1, turn; working in **both** loops of sts on Row 22 **and** in free loops of previous row, sc in each st across; finish off.

# Wavy Cowl

DESIGN BY KAREN WHOOLEY

■■□□ **EASY**

**FINISHED SIZE**

5¾" wide x 60½" circumference
(14.5 cm x 153.5 cm)

**GAUGE**

In pattern,
one repeat (17 sts) = 5½" (14 cm);
8 rows = 4" (10 cm)

**Gauge Swatch:** 11" wide x 4" high
(28 cm x 10 cm)

Ch 37.
Work same as Cowl through Row 8,
page 13: 34 sc.

Each row is worked across the length
of the Cowl.

## SHOPPING LIST

**Yarn** (Medium Weight)
[7 ounces, 426 yards
(197 grams, 389 meters) per skein]:

☐ White - 1 skein

☐ Blue - 20 yards (18.5 meters)

☐ Green - 20 yards (18.5 meters)

☐ Purple - 20 yards (18.5 meters)

☐ Pink - 20 yards (18.5 meters)

☐ Yellow - 20 yards (18.5 meters)

## Crochet Hook

☐ Size J (6 mm)

**or** size needed for gauge

## Additional Supplies

☐ Yarn needle

## STRIPE SEQUENCE

One row **each** of White, Blue, White, Green, White, Purple, White, Pink, White, Yellow, White.

- - - - - - - - - - - - - - - - - - - - - - - -

## COWL

With White, ch 190.

**Row 1** (Right side)**:** Working in back ridge of beginning ch *(Fig. 2, page 62)*, dc in fourth ch from hook **(3 skipped chs count as first dc)**, 2 dc in each of next 2 chs, (skip next ch, dc in next ch) 5 times, ★ skip next ch, 2 dc in each of next 6 chs, (skip next ch, dc in next ch) 5 times; repeat from ★ across to last 4 chs, skip next ch, 2 dc in each of last 3 chs; finish off: 187 dc.

*Note:* Loop a short piece of yarn around any stitch to mark Row 1 as **right** side.

**Row 2:** With **wrong** side facing, join next color with sc in first dc *(see Joining With Sc, page 61)*; sc in each dc across; finish off.

**Row 3:** With **right** side facing and working in Back Loops Only *(Fig. 3, page 62)*, join White with dc in first sc *(see Joining With Dc, page 61)*; dc in same st, 2 dc in each of next 2 sc, (skip next sc, dc in next sc) 5 times, ★ skip next sc, 2 dc in each of next 6 sc, (skip next sc, dc in next sc) 5 times; repeat from ★ across to last 4 sc, skip next sc, 2 dc in each of last 3 sc; finish off.

**Rows 4-11:** Repeat Rows 2 and 3, 4 times.

With **right** side together, sew short ends of Cowl together.

# Flower Mug Cozy

DESIGN BY MICHELE WILCOX

 **EASY**

**FINISHED SIZE**

2¼" high x 10" long
(5.75 cm x 25.5 cm)
(excluding Button Loops)

**GAUGE**

In Cozy pattern,
(sc, dc) 3 times = 1¾" (4.5 cm);
5 rows = 1⁵/₈" (4 cm)

**Gauge Swatch:**

2¼" wide x 2" long (5.75 cm x 5 cm)
Work same as Cozy thru Row 5,
page 16: 8 sts.

## SHOPPING LIST

### Yarn (Medium Weight) 🧶4

[7 ounces, 364 yards
(198 grams, 333 meters) per skein]:

☐ White - 25 yards (23 meters)

☐ Pink - 5 yards (4.5 meters)

☐ Green - 5 yards (4.5 meters)

### Crochet Hook

☐ Size G (4 mm)

**or** size needed for gauge

### Additional Supplies

☐ Yarn needle

☐ Sewing needle and thread

☐ ½" (12 mm) buttons - 4

# Flower Mug Cozy

## STITCH GUIDE

**TREBLE CROCHET** *(abbreviated tr)*
YO twice, insert hook in sc indicated, YO and pull up a loop (4 loops on hook), (YO and draw through 2 loops on hook) 3 times.

- - - - - - - - - - - - - - - - - - - - - - - - - - -

## COZY

With White, ch 11.

**Row 1** (Right side)**:** Dc in third ch from hook, skip next ch, ★ (sc, dc) in next ch, skip next ch; repeat from ★ 2 times **more**, sc in last ch: 8 sts.

*Note:* Loop a short piece of yarn around any stitch to mark Row 1 as **right** side.

**Row 2:** Ch 1, turn; dc in first sc, skip next dc, ★ (sc, dc) in next sc, skip next dc; repeat from ★ 2 times **more**, sc in top of beginning ch.

**Rows 3-31:** Ch 1, turn; dc in first sc, skip next dc, ★ (sc, dc) in next sc, skip next dc; repeat from ★ 2 times **more**, sc in turning ch-1; at end of Row 31, finish off.

**Row 32** (Button Loops)**:** With **right** side facing, join White with slip st in first dc; ch 5, slip st in same st, sc in next 2 sts, (slip st, ch 5, slip st) in next sc, sc in next 2 sts, slip st in next dc, ch 5, slip st in last sc, finish off.

# FLOWER
## Center

**Rnd 1** (Right side)**:** With Pink, ch 2, 6 sc in second ch from hook; join with slip st to Front Loop Only of first sc *(Fig. 3, page 62)*.

*Note:* Mark Rnd 1 as **right** side.

**Rnd 2:** Ch 1, working in Front Loops Only, 3 sc in same st, (slip st, ch 1, 3 sc) in next sc and in each sc around; join with slip st to free loop of first sc *(Fig. 4a, page 62)*: 6 petals.

**Rnd 3:** Ch 1, working **behind** petals in free loops of sc on Rnd 1, 2 sc in same st as joining and in each sc around; join with slip st to Front Loop Only of first sc: 12 sc.

**Rnd 4:** Ch 1, working in Front Loops Only, 3 dc in next sc, ch 1, ★ slip st in next sc, ch 1, 3 dc in next sc, ch 1; repeat from ★ around; join with slip st to first slip st, finish off: 6 petals.

**Rnd 5:** With **right** side facing and working in free loops of sc on Rnd 3, join Green with sc in first sc *(see Joining With Sc, page 61)*; 2 sc in next sc, (sc in next sc, 2 sc in next sc) around; join with slip st to Front Loop Only of first sc: 18 sc.

**Rnd 6:** Working in Front Loops Only, ch 1, dc in same st as joining, 3 tr in next sc, dc in next sc, ch 1, ★ (slip st, ch 1, dc) in next sc, 3 tr in next sc, dc in next sc, ch 1; repeat from ★ around; join with slip st to **both** loops of first slip st, finish off leaving a long end for sewing.

With **right** sides of both pieces facing and using photo as a guide for placement, sew Flower to Cozy; then sew button to Flower Center.

Sew buttons opposite button loops, adjusting placement for your mug.

# Floral Marketbag

DESIGN BY LINDA A. DALEY

 **EASY**

FINISHED SIZE
13½" wide x 19" high
(34.5 cm x 48.5 cm)
(excluding handles)

GAUGE
First Motif = 3¼" (8.25 cm) square
11 sc = 2" (5 cm)

**Gauge Swatch:**
2½" (6.25 cm) diameter
Work same as First Motif thru Flower,
page 20: 8 Clusters and 8 ch-5 sps.

## SHOPPING LIST

**Yarn** (Fine Weight)
[3.5 ounces, 317 yards
(100 grams, 290 meters) per ball]:
☐ Main Color (White) - 2 balls
*Note:* Each Motif requires approximately
9 yards (8.25 meters) of Main Color.
☐ Contrasting Color -1 ball **total** of
4 colors - Blue, Purple, Peach, and Green
*Note:* Each Flower requires approximately
6 yards **total** (5.5 meters).

## Crochet Hook
☐ Size F (3.75 mm)
   **or** size needed for gauge

## Additional Supplies
☐ Safety pin
☐ Tapestry needle

# Floral Marketbag

## STITCH GUIDE

### BEGINNING CLUSTER

(uses one ch-2 sp)

Ch 2, ★ YO, insert hook in **same** sp, YO and pull up a loop, YO and draw through 2 loops on hook; repeat from ★ 2 times **more**, YO and draw through all 4 loops on hook.

### CLUSTER (uses one ch-2 sp)

★ YO, insert hook in ch-2 sp indicated, YO and pull up a loop, YO and draw through 2 loops on hook; repeat from ★ 3 times **more**, YO and draw through all 5 loops on hook.

- - - - - - - - - - - - - - - - - - -

## FIRST MOTIF
### Flower

With Contrasting Color, ch 6; join with slip st to form a ring.

**Rnd 1** (Right side)**:** Ch 5 (**counts as first dc plus ch 2**), (dc in ring, ch 2) 7 times; join with slip st to first dc, do **not** finish off for Solid Flower **OR** finish off to make a Two-Color Flower: 8 dc and 8 ch-2 sps.

*Note:* Loop a short piece of yarn around any stitch to mark Rnd 1 as **right** side.

**Solid Flower ONLY - Rnd 2:** Slip st in next ch-2 sp, work Beginning Cluster, ch 5, (work Cluster in next ch-2 sp, ch 5) around; join with slip st to top of Beginning Cluster, finish off: 8 Clusters and 8 ch-5 sps.

**Two-Color Flower ONLY - Rnd 2:** With **right** side facing, join next Contrasting Color with slip st in any ch-2 sp; work Beginning Cluster, ch 5, (work Cluster in next ch-2 sp, ch 5) around; join with slip st to top of Beginning Cluster, finish off: 8 Clusters and 8 ch-5 sps.

## Border

**Rnd 1:** With **right** side facing, join Main Color with sc in top of any Cluster (*see Joining With Sc, page 61*); ch 2, dc in next dc on Rnd 1 working **around** ch-5 (*Fig. 7, page 63*), ch 2, ★ sc in top of next Cluster, ch 2, dc in next dc on Rnd 1 working **around** ch-5, ch 2; repeat from ★ around; join with slip st to first sc: 16 ch-2 sps.

**Rnd 2:** (Slip st, ch 1, sc) in next ch-2 sp, ch 3, (sc in next ch-2 sp, ch 3) around; join with slip st to first sc.

**Rnd 3:** Slip st in next ch-3 sp, ch 3 (**counts as first dc, now and throughout**), (dc, ch 2, 2 dc) in same sp, ch 2, sc in next ch-3 sp, (ch 3, sc in next ch-3 sp) twice, ch 2, ★ (2 dc, ch 2) twice in next ch-3 sp, sc in next ch-3 sp, (ch 3, sc in next ch-3 sp) twice, ch 2; repeat from ★ 2 times **more**; join with slip st to first dc, finish off: 20 sps.

## NEXT 39 MOTIFS

The method used to connect the Motifs is a no-sew joining also known as "join-as-you-go". After the first Motif is made, each remaining Motif is worked to the last round, then crocheted together as the last round is worked. Holding pieces with **wrong** sides together, sc in space as indicated.

Work same as First Motif through Border Rnd 2: 16 ch-3 sps.

**Rnd 3** (Joining rnd)**:** Referring to Diagram, work One Side, Opposite Side, Two Side, or Three Side Joining.

### DIAGRAM

| S | T | S | T | S | T | S | T |
|---|---|---|---|---|---|---|---|
| T | S | T | S | T | S | T | S |
| S | T | S | T | S | T | S | T |
| T | S | T | S | T | S | T | S |
| S | T | S | T | S | T | S | T |

### KEY
S - Solid Flower
T - Two-Color Flower

*Note:* Dotted lines represent joined edges.

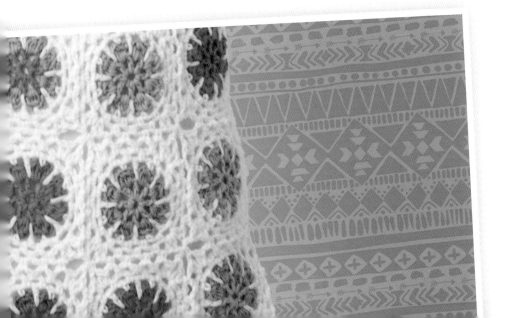

## One Side Joining

**Rnd 3:** (Slip st, ch 3, dc) in next ch-3 sp, ch 1; with **wrong** sides together, sc in corresponding corner ch-2 sp on **previous Motif**, ch 1, 2 dc in same sp on **new Motif**, ch 1, sc in next ch-2 sp on **previous Motif**, ch 1, sc in next ch-3 sp on **new Motif**, (ch 2, sc in next ch-3 sp on **previous Motif**, ch 1, sc in next ch-3 sp on **new Motif**) twice, ch 1, sc in next ch-2 sp on **previous Motif**, ch 1, 2 dc in next ch-3 sp on **new Motif**, ch 1, sc in next corner ch-2 sp on **previous Motif**, ch 1, 2 dc in same sp on **new Motif**, ch 2, sc in next ch-3 sp, (ch 3, sc in next ch-3 sp) twice, ch 2, ★ (2 dc, ch 2) twice in next ch-3 sp, sc in next ch-3 sp, (ch 3, sc in next ch-3 sp) twice, ch 2; repeat from ★ once **more**; join with slip st to first dc, finish off.

When joining to a previously joined corner, sc in same sp.

## Opposite Side Joining

**Rnd 3:** (Slip st, ch 3, dc) in next ch-3 sp, ch 1; with **wrong** sides together, sc in corresponding corner ch-2 sp on **previous Motif**, ch 1, 2 dc in same sp on **new Motif**, ch 1, sc in next ch-2 sp on **previous Motif**, ch 1, sc in next ch-3 sp on **new Motif**, (ch 2, sc in next ch-3 sp on **previous Motif**, ch 1, sc in next ch-3 sp on **new Motif**) twice, ch 1, sc in next ch-2 sp on **previous Motif**, ch 1, 2 dc in next ch-3 sp on **new Motif**, ch 1, sc in next corner ch-2 sp on **previous Motif**, ch 1, 2 dc in same sp on **new Motif**, ch 2, sc in next ch-3 sp, (ch 3, sc in next ch-3 sp) twice, ch 2, 2 dc in next ch-3 sp, ch 1; with **wrong** side facing and being careful not to twist piece, sc in corresponding corner ch-2 sp on **opposite Motif**, ch 1, 2 dc in same sp on **new Motif**, ch 1, sc in next ch-2 sp on **opposite Motif**, ch 1, sc in next ch-3 sp on **new Motif**, (ch 2, sc in next ch-3 sp on **opposite Motif**, ch 1, sc in next ch-3 sp on **new Motif**) twice, ch 1, sc in next ch-2 sp on **opposite Motif**, ch 1, 2 dc in next ch-3 sp on **new Motif**, ch 1, sc in next corner ch-2 sp on **opposite Motif**, ch 1, 2 dc in same sp on **new Motif**, ch 2, sc in next ch-3 sp, (ch 3, sc in next ch-3 sp) twice, ch 2; join with slip st to first dc, finish off.

# Floral Marketbag

## Two Side Joining

**Rnd 3:** (Slip st, ch 3, dc) in next ch-3 sp, ch 1; with **wrong** sides together, sc in corresponding corner ch-2 sp on **previous** Motif, ch 1, 2 dc in same sp on **new Motif**, ch 1, sc in next ch-2 sp on **previous Motif**, ch 1, sc in next ch-3 sp on **new Motif**, (ch 2, sc in next ch-3 sp on **previous Motif**, ch 1, sc in next ch-3 sp on **new Motif**) twice, ch 1, sc in next ch-2 sp on **previous Motif**, ch 1, 2 dc in next ch-3 sp on **new Motif**, ch 1, sc in next corner ch-2 sp on **adjacent** Motif, ch 1, 2 dc in same sp on **new** Motif, ch 1, sc in next ch-2 sp on **adjacent Motif**, ch 1, sc in next ch-3 sp on **new Motif**, (ch 2, sc in next ch-3 sp on **adjacent Motif**, ch 1, sc in next ch-3 sp on **new Motif**) twice, ch 1, sc in next ch-2 sp on **adjacent Motif**, ch 1, 2 dc in next ch-3 sp on **new Motif**, ch 1, sc in next corner ch-2 sp on **adjacent Motif**, ch 1, 2 dc in same sp on **new Motif**, ch 2, sc in next ch-3 sp, (ch 3, sc in next ch-3 sp) twice, ch 2, (2 dc, ch 2) twice in next ch-3 sp, sc in next ch-3 sp, (ch 3, sc in next ch-3 sp) twice, ch 2; join with slip st to first dc, finish off.

## Three Side Joining

**Rnd 3:** (Slip st, ch 3, dc) in next ch-3 sp, ch 1; with **wrong** sides together, sc in corresponding corner ch-2 sp on **previous** Motif, ch 1, 2 dc in same sp on **new Motif**, ch 1, sc in next ch-2 sp on **previous Motif**, ch 1, sc in next ch-3 sp on **new Motif**, (ch 2, sc in next ch-3 sp on **previous Motif**, ch 1, sc in next ch-3 sp on **new Motif**) twice, ch 1, sc in next ch-2 sp on **previous Motif**, ch 1, 2 dc in next ch-3 sp on **new Motif**, ch 1, sc in next corner ch-2 sp on **adjacent** Motif, ch 1, 2 dc in same sp on **new Motif**, ★ ch 1, sc in next ch-2 sp on **adjacent Motif**, ch 1, sc in next ch-3 sp on **new Motif**, (ch 2, sc in next ch-3 sp on **adjacent Motif**, ch 1, sc in next ch-3 sp on **new Motif**) twice, ch 1, sc in next ch-2 sp on **adjacent Motif**, ch 1, 2 dc in next ch-3 sp on **new Motif**, ch 1, sc in next corner ch-2 sp on **adjacent Motif**, ch 1, 2 dc in same sp on **new Motif**; repeat from ★ once **more**, ch 2, sc in next ch-3 sp, (ch 3, sc in next ch-3 sp) twice, ch 2; join with slip st to first dc, finish off.

## EDGINGS

### Bottom

**Rnd 1:** With **right** side facing, join Main Color with sc in first corner sp of any Motif; (ch 3, sc in next sp) around, ch 1, hdc in first sc to form last ch-3 sp: 48 ch-3 sps.

**Rnd 2:** Ch 1, 2 sc in last ch-3 sp made, 3 sc in each ch-3 sp around, sc in same sp as first sc; join with slip st to first sc, finish off leaving a long end for sewing: 144 sc.

### Top

**Rnds 1 and 2:** Work same as Bottom Edging, joining Main Color with sc in corner sp of corresponding Motif on top edge; at end of Rnd 2, do **not** finish off: 144 sc.

**Rnds 3 and 4:** Ch 1, sc in same st as joining and in each sc around; join with slip st to first sc.

**Rnd 5:** Ch 1, sc in same st as joining, ch 1, skip next sc, ★ sc in next sc, ch 1, skip next sc; repeat from ★ around; join with slip st to first sc, place loop from hook onto safety pin to keep piece from unraveling while working the next round, keep yarn and loop on **wrong** side of work: 72 sc and 72 chs.

**Rnd 6:** With **right** side facing and working **around** chs, join Contrasting Color (Green) with hdc in first skipped sc on Rnd 4 *(see Joining With Hdc, page 61)*; ch 1, skip next sc on Rnd 5, ★ hdc in next skipped sc on Rnd 4, ch 1, skip next sc on Rnd 5; repeat from ★ around; join with slip st to first hdc, finish off.

**Rnd 7:** With **right** side facing, place loop from safety pin onto hook (loop will be **behind** Rnd 6); ch 1, working **around** chs, hdc in same st as joining on Rnd 5, sc in next hdc on Rnd 6, (hdc in next skipped sc on Rnd 5, sc in next hdc on Rnd 6) around; join with slip st to first hdc: 144 sts.

**Rnds 8 and 9:** Ch 1, sc in same st as joining and in each st around; join with slip st to first sc.

**Rnd 10:** Ch 1, sc in same st as joining and in next 16 sc, place marker in last sc made for first handle placement, sc in next 72 sc, place marker in last sc made for second handle placement, sc in each sc around; join with slip st to first sc, finish off.

## FINISHING
### Handles

**Row 1:** With **right** side of Top Edging facing, join Main Color with slip st in first marked sc on Rnd 10; ch 110, skip next 44 sc, slip st in next 2 sc, **turn**; working in back ridge of chs *(Fig. 2, page 62)*, sc in each ch across, with **wrong** side facing, slip st in next 2 sc on Top Edging: 110 sc.

**Row 2:** Turn; skip first 2 slip sts, sc in each sc across; with **right** side facing, slip st in next 2 sc on Top Edging.

**Row 3:** Turn; skip first 2 slip sts, sc in each sc across; with **wrong** side facing, slip st in next 2 sc on Top Edging.

**Rows 4-7:** Repeat Rnds 2 and 3 twice.

**Row 8:** Turn; skip first 2 slip sts, sc in each sc across; slip st in next sc on Top Edging; finish off.

Beginning in second marked sc on Rnd 10 of Top Edging, repeat for second Handle.

With **wrong** side together and working through **both** loops of **both** layers, sew bottom seam using long end.

# Vibrant Mandala

DESIGN BY SUE GALUCKI

■■□□ **EASY**

**FINISHED SIZE**

22" (56 cm) diameter

**GAUGE**

Rnds 1 and 2 = 3" (7.5 cm) diameter

**Gauge Swatch:**

3" (7.5 cm) diameter

Work same as Body through Rnd 2, page 26: 42 dc.

## SHOPPING LIST

### Yarn (Medium Weight)

[6 ounces, 315 yards
(170 grams, 288 meters) per skein]:

☐ White - 100 yards (91.5 meters)

☐ Blue - 100 yards (91.5 meters)

☐ Aqua - 65 yards (59.5 meters)

☐ Pink - 50 yards (45.5 meters)

☐ Orange - 35 yards (32 meters)

### Crochet Hook

☐ Size H (5 mm)

**or** size needed for gauge

### Additional Supplies

☐ 23" (58.5 cm) diameter quilting hoop

☐ White spray paint

☐ Yarn needle

# Vibrant Mandala

## BODY

With White, ch 7; join with slip st to form a ring.

**Rnd 1** (Right side)**:** Ch 5 (**counts as first dc plus ch 2, now and throughout**), (dc in ring, ch 2) 13 times; join with slip st to first dc: 14 dc and 14 ch-2 sps.

*Note:* Loop a short piece of yarn around any stitch to mark Rnd 1 as **right** side.

**Rnd 2:** Ch 3 (**counts as first dc, now and throughout**), 2 dc in next ch-2 sp, (dc in next dc, 2 dc in next ch-2 sp) around; join with slip st to first dc changing to Aqua *(Fig. 5d, page 63)*: 42 dc.

**Rnd 3:** Ch 1, sc in sp **before** joining *(Fig. 6, page 63)*, ★ ch 3, skip next 3 dc, sc in sp **before** next dc; repeat from ★ around to last 3 dc, ch 1, skip last 3 dc, hdc in first sc to form last ch-3 sp: 14 ch-3 sps.

**Rnd 4:** Ch 1, 2 sc in last ch-3 sp made, (ch 3, 2 sc in next ch-3 sp) around, ch 1, hdc in first sc to form last ch-3 sp.

**Rnd 5:** Ch 5, dc in last ch-3 sp made, ch 2, (dc, ch 2) twice in next ch-3 sp and in each ch-3 sp around; join with slip st to first dc changing to Blue: 28 ch-2 sps.

**Rnd 6:** Slip st in next ch-2 sp, ch 6 (**counts as first dc plus ch 3, now and throughout**), (dc in next ch-2 sp, ch 3) around; join with slip st to first dc.

**Rnd 7:** (Slip st, ch 3, 3 dc) in next ch-3 sp, 4 dc in next ch-3 sp and in each ch-3 sp around; join with slip st to first dc changing to Pink: 112 dc.

**Rnd 8:** Ch 1, sc in sp **before** joining, ch 7, skip next 4 dc, ★ sc in sp **before** next dc, ch 7, skip next 4 dc; repeat from ★ around; join with slip st to first sc: 28 ch-7 sps.

**Rnd 9:** (Slip st, ch 3, 8 dc) in next ch-7 sp, sc in next ch-7 sp, ★ 9 dc in next ch-7 sp, sc in next ch-7 sp; repeat from ★ around; join with slip st to first dc changing to White: 140 sts.

**Rnd 10:** Ch 1, sc in same st as joining, (ch 4, skip next 3 dc, sc in next dc) twice, ★ ch 4, skip next sc, sc in next dc, (ch 4, skip next 3 dc, sc in next dc) twice; repeat from ★ around to last sc, ch 1, skip last sc, dc in first sc to form last ch-4 sp: 42 ch-4 sps.

**Rnd 11:** Ch 5, dc in last ch-4 sp made, ch 2, (dc, ch 2) twice in next ch-4 sp and in each ch-4 sp around; join with slip st to first dc changing to Orange: 84 ch-2 sps.

**Rnd 12:** Slip st in next ch-2 sp, ch 6, skip next ch-2 sp, dc in next ch-2 sp, ★ ch 3, skip next ch-2 sp, dc in next ch-2 sp; repeat from ★ around to last ch-2 sp, ch 1, skip last ch-2 sp, hdc in first dc to form last ch-3 sp: 42 ch-3 sps.

**Rnd 13:** Ch 3, dc in last ch-3 sp made, ch 1, ★ (2 dc, ch 2, 2 dc) in next ch-3 sp, ch 1; repeat from ★ around, 2 dc in same sp as first dc, ch 1, sc in first dc to form last ch-2 sp changing to Aqua *(Fig. 5a, page 63)*: 84 sps.

**Rnd 14:** Ch 3, dc in last ch-2 sp made, sc in next ch-1 sp, ★ (2 dc, ch 2, 2 dc) in next ch-2 sp, sc in next ch-1 sp; repeat from ★ around, 2 dc in same sp as first dc, ch 1, sc in first dc to form last ch-2 sp changing to White: 42 ch-2 sps.

**Rnd 15:** Ch 3, dc in last ch-2 sp made, ch 1, (2 dc, ch 1) twice in next ch-2 sp and in each ch-2 sp around, 2 dc in same sp as first dc, sc in first dc to form last ch-1 sp changing to Pink: 84 ch-1 sps.

**Rnd 16:** Ch 3, dc in last ch-1 sp made, sc in next ch-1 sp, ★ (2 dc, ch 2, 2 dc) in next ch-1 sp, sc in next ch-1 sp; repeat from ★ around, 2 dc in same sp as first dc, ch 1, sc in first dc to form last ch-2 sp changing to Blue: 42 ch-2 sps.

**Rnd 17:** Ch 3, dc in last ch-2 sp made, ch 1, ★ (2 dc, ch 2, 2 dc) in next ch-2 sp, ch 1; repeat from ★ around, 2 dc in same sp as first dc, ch 1, sc in first dc to form last ch-2 sp changing to White: 84 sps.

**Rnd 18:** Ch 3, dc in last ch-2 sp made, sc in next ch-1 sp, ★ (2 dc, ch 2, 2 dc) in next ch-2 sp, sc in next ch-1 sp; repeat from ★ around, 2 dc in same sp as first dc, ch 1, sc in first dc to form last ch-2 sp changing to Aqua: 42 ch-2 sps.

**Rnd 19:** Ch 3, dc in last ch-2 sp made, ch 2, (2 dc, ch 2) twice in next ch-2 sp and in each ch-2 sp around, 2 dc in same sp as first dc, ch 1, sc in first dc to form last ch-2 sp changing to Blue: 84 ch-2 sps.

**Rnd 20:** Ch 3, dc in last ch-2 sp made, ch 1, sc in next ch-2 sp, ch 1, ★ (2 dc, ch 2, 2 dc) in next ch-2 sp, ch 1, sc in next ch-2 sp, ch 1; repeat from ★ around, 2 dc in same sp as first dc, ch 1, sc in first dc to form last ch-2 sp: 210 sts and 126 sps.

**Rnd 21:** Ch 1, sc in last ch-2 sp made and in next 2 dc and next ch-1 sp, skip next sc, sc in next ch-1 sp and in next 2 dc, ★ (sc, ch 3, sc) in next ch-2 sp, sc in next 2 dc and in next ch-1 sp, skip next sc, sc in next ch-1 sp and in next 2 dc; repeat from ★ around, sc in same sp as first sc, ch 3; join with slip st to first sc, finish off.

## FINISHING

Spray paint inside hoop of quilting hoop, let dry completely.

Cut 2, 72" (183 cm) lengths of Blue.
Thread yarn needle with both strands of Blue. Using photo as a guide, weave yarn through ch-3 sps on Rnd 21 and around hoop to secure Body to hoop. Knot ends behind Body to secure ends; then weave in ends.

# Daisies Notebook Cover

**◼◼◻◻ EASY**

## FINISHED SIZE

11½" (29 cm) high

## GAUGE

In Body pattern, 18 sc = 4" (10 cm)

In Flap pattern,

18 sts (chs and sc) and

21 rows = 4" (10 cm)

**Gauge Swatch:** 4" (10 cm) square

With Main Color, ch 19.

**Row 1:** Sc in back ridge of second ch from hook and each ch across (**Fig. 2, page 62**): 18 sc.

**Row 2:** Ch 1, turn; sc in first sc, ch 1, (skip next sc, sc in next sc, ch 1) across to last 3 sc, skip next sc, sc in last 2 sc: 10 sc and 8 ch-1 sps.

**Rows 3-21:** Ch 1, turn; sc in first sc, (ch 1, sc in next ch-1 sp) across to last sc, sc in last sc.

Finish off.

## SHOPPING LIST

### Yarn

**COVER**

(Light Weight)

[5.3 ounces, 590 yards,

(150 grams, 540 meters) per skein]:

☐ Main Color - 2 skeins

**DAISIES AND LEAVES**

(Medium Weight)

*Note:* Yardages are for one Daisy or one Leaf of each size.

**Large Daisy**
- ☐ White - 15 yards (13.5 meters)
- ☐ Yellow - 4 yards (3.5 meters)

**Small Daisy**
- ☐ White - 8 yards (7.5 meters)
- ☐ Yellow - 3 yards (2.5 meters)

**Small Leaf**
- ☐ Green - 4 yards (3.5 meters)

**Large Leaf**
- ☐ Green - 5 yards (4.5 meters)

# Crochet Hook
- ☐ Size G (4 mm)

   **or** size needed for gauge

# Additional Supplies
- ☐ Sewing pins
- ☐ Yarn needle
- ☐ Polyester fiberfill

# COVER
## Body

With Main Color, ch 48.

**Row 1** (Wrong side)**:** Sc in back ridge of second ch from hook and each ch across *(Fig. 2, page 62)*: 47 sc.

*Note:* Loop a short piece of yarn around the **back** of any stitch on Row 1 to mark **right** side.

**Row 2:** Ch 1, turn; working in Back Loops Only of sc on Row 1 **and** in one free loop of beginning ch *(Fig. A, page 11)*, sc in each st across.

**Row 3:** Ch 1, turn; working in Back Loops Only of sts on last row **and** in free loops of previous row *(Fig. B, page 11)*, sc in each st across.

# Daisies Notebook Cover

Repeat Row 3 for pattern until piece measures ¾" (1.9 cm) less than width of opened notebook ending by working a **wrong** side row. Our model fits a notebook with a 1" (2.5 cm) spine.

**Last Row:** Ch 1, turn; working in **both** loops of sts on last row **and** in free loops of previous row, sc in each st across; finish off.

**Trim:** With **right** side facing, join Main Color with sc in any sc on Last Row of Body *(see Joining With Sc, page 61)*; sc evenly around entire piece working 3 sc in each corner; join with slip st to first sc, finish off.

## Flap (Make 2)
With Main Color, ch 41.

**Row 1** (Right side)**:** Sc in back ridge of second ch from hook and each ch across: 40 sc.

*Note:* Mark Row 1 as **right** side.

**Row 2:** Ch 1, turn; sc in first sc, ch 1, (skip next sc, sc in next sc, ch 1) across to last 3 sc, skip next sc, sc in last 2 sc: 21 sc and 19 ch-1 sps.

**Rows 3-50:** Ch 1, turn; sc in first sc, (ch 1, sc in next ch-1 sp) across to last sc, sc in last sc.

**Row 51:** Ch 1, turn; sc in each sc and each ch-1 sp across; finish off: 40 sc.

With **wrong** sides together, pin each Flap to Body, stretching Flaps to fit.

**Edging:** With **right** side facing and working in ends of rows, join Main Color with sc in first row on inner edge; sc evenly across, finish off.
Repeat for remaining Flap.

## Joining

With **right** side of Body facing and working through **both** layers, join Main Color with sc in center sc of any corner 3-sc group; sc in each st around working 3 sc in center sc of each corner 3-sc group; join with slip st to first sc, finish off.

# Daisies Notebook Cover

## DAISIES & LEAVES

DESIGNS BY AMY GAINES

### GAUGE

Gauge is not of great importance; your Daisies and Leaves may be a little larger or smaller without changing the overall effect.

### Large Daisy

#### PETALS

**Rnd 1** (Right side)**:** With White, make an adjustable loop to form a ring *(Figs. 1a-d, page 62)*, work 6 sc in ring; do **not** join, place marker to indicate beginning of rnd *(see Markers, page 60)*.

*Note:* Mark Rnd 1 as **right** side.

**Rnd 2:** 2 Sc in each sc around: 12 sc.

**Rnd 3:** (2 Sc in next sc, sc in next sc) around: 18 sc.

**Rnd 4:** ★ Ch 7; sc in second ch from hook and in next ch, hdc in next 2 chs, sc in last 2 chs, sc in next sc on Rnd 3; repeat from ★ around; slip st in first ch of first petal, finish off: 18 petals.

#### CENTER

**Rnds 1-3:** With Yellow, work same as Petals: 18 sc.

**Rnd 4:** Sc in each sc around; slip st in next sc, finish off leaving a long end for sewing.

With long end, sew Center to Rnd 3 of Petals, stuffing with polyester fiberfill before closing; do not **cut** yarn.

### Small Daisy

#### PETALS

**Rnd 1** (Right side)**:** With White, make an adjustable loop to form a ring, work 6 sc in ring; do **not** join, place marker to indicate beginning of rnd.

*Note:* Mark Rnd 1 as **right** side.

**Rnd 2:** 2 Sc in each sc around: 12 sc.

**Rnd 3:** ★ Ch 5; sc in second ch from hook, hdc in next 2 chs, sc in last ch, sc in next sc on Rnd 2; repeat from ★ around; slip st in first ch of first petal, finish off: 12 petals.

#### CENTER

**Rnds 1 and 2:** With Yellow, work same as Petals: 12 sc.

**Rnd 3:** Sc in each sc around; slip st in next sc, finish off leaving a long end for sewing.

With long end, sew Center to Rnd 2 of Petals, stuffing with polyester fiberfill before closing; do not **cut** yarn.

## LEAVES
### Small Leaf
With Green and leaving a long end for sewing, ch 8.

**Rnd 1** (Right side)**:** 3 Dc in fourth ch from hook, dc in next ch, hdc in next ch, sc in next ch, (sc, ch 1, sc) in last ch; working in free loops of beginning ch *(Fig. 4b, page 62)*, sc in next ch, hdc in next ch, dc in next ch, 3 dc in next ch; join with slip st to first st; ch 9 (stem), slip st in second ch from hook and in each ch across; finish off.

*Note:* Mark Rnd 1 as **right** side.

### Large Leaf
With Green and leaving a long end for sewing, ch 7.

**Rnd 1** (Right side)**:** 2 Sc in second ch from hook, hdc in next 3 chs, sc in next ch, 3 sc in last ch; working in free loops of beginning ch, sc in next ch, hdc in next 3 chs, 2 sc in next ch; join with slip st to first sc: 15 sts.

*Note:* Mark Rnd 1 as **right** side.

**Rnd 2:** Ch 1, 2 sc in same st as joining, hdc in next sc, 2 dc in each of next 2 hdc, hdc in next 2 sts, sc in next sc, (sc, ch 2, sc) in next sc, sc in next sc, hdc in next 2 sts, 2 dc in each of next 2 hdc, hdc in next sc, 2 sc in last sc; join with slip st to first sc; ch 11 (stem), slip st in second ch from hook and in each ch across; finish off.

Using photo as a guide for placement and long ends, sew Daisies and Leaves to Cover.

# Oval Rug

## DESIGN BY MAGGIE WELDON

**EASY**

**FINISHED SIZE**

25½" wide x 37" long
(65 cm x 94 cm)

**GAUGE**

10 dc = 7" (18 cm)

**Gauge Swatch:** 6" wide x 16" long
(15.25 cm x 40.5 cm)

Work same as Body through Rnd 2,
page 36: 48 dc.

## SHOPPING LIST

**Yarn** (Super Bulky Weight)

[5 ounces, 81 yards
(142 grams, 74 meters) per skein]:

☐ Blue - 4 skeins

☐ Red - 2 skeins

☐ Yellow - 2 skeins

☐ Purple - 2 skeins

☐ Green - 2 skeins

## Crochet Hook

☐ Size N/P (10 mm)

   **or** size needed for gauge

---

## STITCH GUIDE

**V-STITCH** (abbreviated V-St)

(Dc, ch 1, dc) in next dc.

# Oval Rug

## BODY

With Green, ch 17.

**Rnd 1** (Right side)**:** 2 Dc in fourth ch from hook (**3 skipped chs count as first dc**), dc in next 12 chs, 6 dc in last ch; working in free loops of beginning ch (*Fig. 4b, page 62*), dc in next 12 chs, 3 dc in next ch; join with slip st to first dc: 36 dc.

*Note:* Loop a short piece of yarn around any stitch to mark Rnd 1 as **right** side.

**Rnd 2:** Ch 3 (**counts as first dc, now and throughout**), dc in same st as joining, 2 dc in each of next 2 dc, dc in next 12 dc, 2 dc in each of next 6 dc, dc in next 12 dc, 2 dc in each of last 3 dc; join with slip st to first dc, finish off: 48 dc.

**Rnd 3:** With **right** side facing, skip first dc and join Purple with dc in next dc (*see Joining With Dc, page 61*); dc in same st and in next dc, 2 dc in next dc, dc in next dc, 2 dc in next dc, dc in next 13 dc, 2 dc in next dc, (dc in next dc, 2 dc in next dc) 5 times, dc in next 13 dc, (2 dc in next dc, dc in next dc) 3 times; join with slip st to first dc: 60 dc.

**Rnd 4:** Ch 4 (**counts as first dc plus ch 1, now and throughout**), dc in same st as joining (**first V-St made**), (skip next dc, work V-St) twice, (skip next 2 dc, work V-St) 6 times, (skip next dc, work V-St) 6 times, (skip next 2 dc, work V-St) 6 times, skip next dc, (work V-St, skip next dc) 3 times; join with slip st to first dc, finish off: 24 V-Sts.

**Rnd 5:** With **right** side facing, join Yellow with dc in first V-St (ch-1 sp); 3 dc in same sp, 4 dc in each of next 2 V-Sts, 3 dc in each of next 6 V-Sts, 4 dc in each of next 6 V-Sts, 3 dc in each of next 6 V-Sts, 4 dc in each of last 3 V-Sts; join with slip st to first dc: 84 dc.

**Rnd 6:** Ch 3, dc in next dc, 2 dc in next dc, (dc in next 4 dc, 2 dc in next dc) twice, dc in next 16 dc, 2 dc in next dc, (dc in next 4 dc, 2 dc in next dc) 5 times, dc in next 16 dc, 2 dc in next dc, (dc in next 4 dc, 2 dc in next dc) twice, dc in last 2 dc; join with slip st to first dc, finish off: 96 dc.

**Rnd 7:** With **right** side facing, skip first dc and join Red with dc in next dc; 2 dc in next dc, (dc in next 4 dc, 2 dc in next dc) twice, dc in next 22 dc, 2 dc in next dc, (dc in next 4 dc, 2 dc in next dc) 5 times, dc in next 22 dc, 2 dc in next dc, (dc in next 4 dc, 2 dc in next dc) twice, dc in last 3 dc; join with slip st to first dc: 108 dc.

**Rnd 8:** Ch 4, dc in same st as joining (first V-St made), skip next dc, work V-St, (skip next 2 dc, work V-St, skip next dc, work V-St) twice, (skip next 2 dc, work V-St) 9 times, skip next dc, work V-St, (skip next 2 dc, work V-St, skip next dc, work V-St) 5 times, (skip next 2 dc, work V-St) 9 times, skip next dc, work V-St, skip next 2 dc, (work V-St, skip next dc, work V-St, skip next 2 dc) twice; join with slip st to first dc, finish off: 40 V-Sts.

**Rnd 9:** With **right** side facing, join Blue with dc in first V-St; 2 dc in same sp, 4 dc in next V-St, (3 dc in next V-St, 4 dc in next V-St) twice, 3 dc in each of next 9 V-Sts, 4 dc in next V-St, (3 dc in next V-St, 4 dc in next V-St) 5 times, 3 dc in each of next 9 V-Sts, 4 dc in next V-St, (3 dc in next V-St, 4 dc in next V-St) twice; join with slip st to first dc: 132 dc.

**Rnd 10:** Ch 3, dc in next 2 dc, 2 dc in next dc, (dc in next 7 dc, 2 dc in next dc) twice, dc in next 25 dc, 2 dc in next dc, (dc in next 7 dc, 2 dc in next dc) 5 times, dc in next 25 dc, 2 dc in next dc, (dc in next 7 dc, 2 dc in next dc) twice, dc in last 4 dc; join with slip st to first dc, finish off.

## Safety Tip

For best use and safety, we recommend that non-slip rug backing be attached to your rug, especially for use on wood floors.

# Tasseled Pillow

DESIGN BY JOAN BEEBE

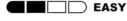 **EASY**

**FINISHED SIZE**

14" (35.5 cm) square

**GAUGE**

Rnds 1 and 2 = 3" (7.5 cm)
(from center tr to center tr)

**Gauge Swatch:** 3" (7.5 cm)
(from center tr to center tr)
Work same as Rnds 1 and 2, page 40:
32 sts.

## SHOPPING LIST

**Yarn** (Light Weight)

[4.5 ounces, 318 yards
(127 grams, 290 meters) per skein]:

☐ White - 1 skein

☐ Green - 100 yards (91 meters)

☐ Pink - 90 yards (82.5 meters)

☐ Blue - 70 yards (64 meters)

☐ Purple - 40 yards (36.5 meters)

## Crochet Hook

☐ Size H (5 mm)

**or** size needed for gauge

## Additional Supplies

☐ Pillow form - 14" (35.5 cm) square

# Tasseled Pillow

## STITCH GUIDE

**TREBLE CROCHET** *(abbreviated tr)*
YO twice, insert hook in st or sp indicated, YO and pull up a loop (4 loops on hook), (YO and draw through 2 loops on hook) 3 times.

— — — — — — — — — — — — — — — — —

## BODY (Make 2)
### COLOR SEQUENCE

One round **each**: Pink, White, Green, White, Purple, White, Blue, White, Pink, White, Green, White.

**Rnd 1** (Right side)**:** With Pink, ch 4 **(3 skipped chs count as first dc)**, 15 dc in fourth ch from hook; join with slip st to first dc, finish off: 16 dc.

*Note:* Loop a short piece of yarn around any stitch to mark Rnd 1 as **right** side.

**Rnd 2:** With **wrong** side facing and working in Back Loops only *(Fig. 2, page 62)*, join White with sc in same st as joining *(see Joining With Sc, page 61)*; skip next dc, 7 tr in next dc, skip next dc, ★ sc in next dc, skip next dc, 7 tr in next dc, skip next dc; repeat from ★ 2 times **more**; join with slip st to Front Loop Only of first sc, finish off: 32 sts.

**Rnd 3:** With **right** side facing and working in Back Loops Only, join Green with sc in center tr of any 7-tr group; (4 tr, ch 3, 4 tr) in next sc (corner made), skip next 3 tr, ★ sc in next tr, (4 tr, ch 3, 4 tr) in next sc (corner made), skip next 3 tr; repeat from ★ 2 times **more**; join with slip st to Front Loop Only of first sc, finish off: 36 sts and 4 corner ch-3 sps.

**Rnd 4:** With **wrong** side facing and working in Back Loops Only, join White with sc in first tr **before** any corner ch-3 sp; (4 tr, ch 3, 4 tr) in corner ch-3 sp, sc in next tr, 7 tr in next sc, skip next 3 tr, ★ sc in next tr, (4 tr, ch 3, 4 tr) in next corner ch-3 sp, sc in next tr, 7 tr in next sc, skip next 3 tr; repeat from ★ 2 times **more**; join with slip st to Front Loop Only of first sc, finish off: 68 sts and 4 corner ch-3 sps.

**Rnd 5:** With **right** side facing and working in Back Loops Only, join next color with tr in any corner ch-3 sp *(see Joining With Tr, page 61)*; (3 tr, ch 3, 4 tr) in same sp, ★ sc in next tr, (7 tr in next sc, skip next 3 tr, sc in next tr) across to next corner ch-3 sp, (4 tr, ch 3, 4 tr) in next corner ch-3 sp; repeat from ★ 2 times **more**, sc in next tr, (7 tr in next sc, skip next 3 tr, sc in next tr) across; join with slip st to first tr, finish off: 100 sts and 4 corner ch-3 sps.

**Rnd 6:** With **wrong** side facing and working in Back Loops Only, join White with tr in any corner ch-3 sp; (3 tr, ch 3, 4 tr) in same sp, ★ sc in next tr, (7 tr in next sc, skip next 3 tr, sc in next tr) across to next corner ch-3 sp, (4 tr, ch 3, 4 tr) in next corner ch-3 sp; repeat from ★ 2 times **more**, sc in next tr, (7 tr in next sc, skip next 3 tr, sc in next tr) across; join with slip st to first tr, finish off: 132 sts and 4 corner ch-3 sps.

**Rnds 7-12:** Repeat Rnds 5 and 6, 3 times: 324 sts and 4 corner ch-3 sps.

## JOINING

With **wrong** sides together, matching sts, and working through **inside** loops of sts on **both** pieces, join White with sc in any corner ch-3 sp; ch 3, sc in same sp and in next tr, ★ (ch 3, sc in next sc, ch 3, skip next 3 tr, sc in next tr) across to next corner ch-3 sp, (sc, ch 3, sc) in corner ch-3 sp, sc in next tr; repeat from ★ 2 times **more**, insert pillow form, (ch 3, sc in next sc, ch 3, skip next 3 tr, sc in next tr) across; join with slip st to first sc, finish off.

**TASSEL** (Make one **each** of Green, Pink, Blue, **and** Purple) Make 5" (12.5 cm) tassel *(Figs. 8a & b, page 63)*, wrapping yarn around cardboard approximately 60 times. Attach one tassel to each corner.

# Ripple Wall Hanging

DESIGN BY KATHLEEN STUART

■■□□ **EASY**

**FINISHED SIZE**

18" wide x 34½" long
(45.5 cm x 87.5 cm)

**GAUGE**

In pattern, one point to point repeat
(11 sts) = 2¼" (5.75 cm);
9 rows = 3" (7.5 cm)

**Gauge Swatch:** 4½" wide x 3¼" high
(11.5 cm x 8.25 cm)

With White, ch 24.

Work same as Body through Row 9,
page 44: 15 sc and 8 ch-1 sps.

Finish off.

## SHOPPING LIST

**Yarn** (Medium Weight)

[6 ounces, 315 yards

(170 grams, 288 meters) per skein]:

☐ White - 1 skein

☐ Green - 90 yards (82.5 meters)

☐ Blue - 85 yards (77.5 meters)

☐ Pink - 80 yards (73 meters)

☐ Orange - 65 yards (59.5 meters)

☐ Yellow - 55 yards (50.5 meters)

## Crochet Hook

☐ Size I (5.5 mm)

**or** size needed for gauge

## Additional Supplies

☐ Round wooden dowel -
¼" diameter x 16" long
(6 mm x 40.5 cm)

☐ Yarn needle

# Ripple Wall Hanging

## BODY

With White, ch 90.

**Row 1** (Right side)**:** Working in back ridge of beginning ch *(Fig. 2, page 62)*, 2 sc in second ch from hook, (ch 1, skip next ch, sc in next ch) twice, skip next 2 chs, (sc in next ch, ch 1, skip next ch) twice, ★ 3 sc in next ch, (ch 1, skip next ch, sc in next ch) twice, skip next 2 chs, (sc in next ch, ch 1, skip next ch) twice; repeat from ★ across to last ch, 2 sc in last ch: 57 sc and 32 ch-1 sps.

*Note:* Loop a short piece of yarn around any stitch to mark Row 1 as **right** side.

**Rows 2-4:** Ch 1, turn; 2 sc in first sc, ch 1, sc in next ch-1 sp, ch 1, sc in next 2 ch-1 sps, ch 1, sc in next ch-1 sp, ch 1, ★ skip next sc, 3 sc in next sc, ch 1, sc in next ch-1 sp, ch 1, sc in next 2 ch-1 sps, ch 1, sc in next ch-1 sp, ch 1; repeat from ★ across to last 2 sc, skip next sc, 2 sc in last sc; at end of Row 4, finish off.

**Row 5:** With **right** side facing, join Green with sc in first sc *(see Joining With Sc, page 61)*; sc in same st, ch 1, sc in next ch-1 sp, ch 1, sc in next 2 ch-1 sps, ch 1, sc in next ch-1 sp, ch 1, ★ skip next sc, 3 sc in next sc, ch 1, sc in next ch-1 sp, ch 1, sc in next 2 ch-1 sps, ch 1, sc in next ch-1 sp, ch 1; repeat from ★ across to last 2 sc, skip next sc, 2 sc in last sc; do **not** finish off.

**Rows 6-8:** Ch 1, turn; 2 sc in first sc, ch 1, sc in next ch-1 sp, ch 1, sc in next 2 ch-1 sps, ch 1, sc in next ch-1 sp, ch 1, ★ skip next sc, 3 sc in next sc, ch 1, sc in next ch-1 sp, ch 1, sc in next 2 ch-1 sps, ch 1, sc in next ch-1 sp, ch 1; repeat from ★ across to last 2 sc, skip next sc, 2 sc in last sc; at end of Row 8, finish off.

**Row 9:** With **right** side facing, join White with sc in first sc; sc in same st, ch 1, sc in next ch-1 sp, ch 1, sc in next 2 ch-1 sps, ch 1, sc in next ch-1 sp, ch 1, ★ skip next sc, 3 sc in next sc, ch 1, sc in next ch-1 sp, ch 1, sc in next 2 ch-1 sps, ch 1, sc in next ch-1 sp, ch 1; repeat from ★ across to last 2 sc, skip next sc, 2 sc in last sc; do **not** finish off.

**Rows 10-12:** Ch 1, turn; 2 sc in first sc, ch 1, sc in next ch-1 sp, ch 1, sc in next 2 ch-1 sps, ch 1, sc in next ch-1 sp, ch 1, ★ skip next sc, 3 sc in next sc, ch 1, sc in next ch-1 sp, ch 1, sc in next 2 ch-1 sps, ch 1, sc in next ch-1 sp, ch 1; repeat from ★ across to last 2 sc, skip next sc, 2 sc in last sc; at end of Row 12, finish off.

**Rows 13-16:** With Pink, repeat Rows 5-8.

**Rows 17-20:** Repeat Rows 9-12.

**Rows 21-24:** With Yellow, repeat Rows 5-8.

**Rows 25-28:** Repeat Rows 9-12.

**Rows 29-32:** With Blue, repeat Rows 5-8.

**Rows 33-36:** Repeat Rows 9-12.

**Rows 37-40:** With Orange, repeat Rows 5-8.

**Rows 41-44:** Repeat Rows 9-12.

**Row 45:** With **right** side facing, join Green with sc in first sc; sc in same st, ch 1, sc in next ch-1 sp, ch 1, sc in next 2 ch-1 sps, ch 1, sc in next ch-1 sp, ch 1, ★ skip next sc, 3 sc in next sc, ch 1, sc in next ch-1 sp, ch 1, sc in next 2 ch-1 sps, ch 1, sc in next ch-1 sp, ch 1; repeat from ★ across to last 2 sc, skip next sc, 2 sc in last sc; do **not** finish off.

**Rows 46 and 47:** Ch 1, turn; 2 sc in first sc, ch 1, sc in next ch-1 sp, ch 1, sc in next 2 ch-1 sps, ch 1, sc in next ch-1 sp, ch 1, ★ skip next sc, 3 sc in next sc, ch 1, sc in next ch-1 sp, ch 1, sc in next 2 ch-1 sps, ch 1, sc in next ch-1 sp, ch 1; repeat from ★ across to last 2 sc, skip next sc, 2 sc in last sc; at end of Row 47, finish off.

**Row 48:** With **wrong** side facing, join White with sc in first sc; sc in same st, ch 1, sc in next ch-1 sp, ch 1, sc in next 2 ch-1 sps, ch 1, sc in next ch-1 sp, ch 1, ★ skip next sc, 3 sc in next sc, ch 1, sc in next ch-1 sp, ch 1, sc in next 2 ch-1 sps, ch 1, sc in next ch-1 sp, ch 1; repeat from ★ across to last 2 sc, skip next sc, 2 sc in last sc; do **not** finish off.

**Rows 49 and 50:** Ch 1, turn; 2 sc in first sc, ch 1, sc in next ch-1 sp, ch 1, sc in next 2 ch-1 sps, ch 1, sc in next ch-1 sp, ch 1, ★ skip next sc, 3 sc in next sc, ch 1, sc in next ch-1 sp, ch 1, sc in next 2 ch-1 sps, ch 1, sc in next ch-1 sp, ch 1; repeat from ★ across to last 2 sc, skip next sc, 2 sc in last sc; at end of Row 51, finish off.

**Rows 51-53:** With Pink, repeat Rows 45-47.

**Rows 54-56:** Repeat Rows 48-50.

**Rows 57-59:** With Yellow, repeat Rows 45-47.

**Rows 60-62:** Repeat Rows 48-50.

**Rows 63-65:** With Blue, repeat Rows 45-47.

**Rows 66-68:** Repeat Rows 48-50.

**Rows 69-71:** With Orange, repeat Rows 45-47.

**Rows 72-74:** Repeat Rows 48-50.

# Ripple Wall Hanging

**Row 75:** With **right** side facing, join Green with sc in first sc; sc in same st, ch 1, sc in next ch-1 sp, ch 1, sc in next 2 ch-1 sps, ch 1, sc in next ch-1 sp, ch 1, ★ skip next sc, 3 sc in next sc, ch 1, sc in next ch-1 sp, ch 1, sc in next 2 ch-1 sps, ch 1, sc in next ch-1 sp, ch 1; repeat from ★ across to last 2 sc, skip next sc, 2 sc in last sc; do **not** finish off.

**Row 76:** Ch 1, turn; 2 sc in first sc, ch 1, sc in next ch-1 sp, ch 1, sc in next 2 ch-1 sps, ch 1, sc in next ch-1 sp, ch 1, ★ skip next sc, 3 sc in next sc, ch 1, sc in next ch-1 sp, ch 1, sc in next 2 ch-1 sps, ch 1, sc in next ch-1 sp, ch 1; repeat from ★ across to last 2 sc, skip next sc, 2 sc in last sc; finish off.

**Row 77:** With **right** side facing, join White with sc in first sc; sc in same st, ch 1, sc in next ch-1 sp, ch 1, sc in next 2 ch-1 sps, ch 1, sc in next ch-1 sp, ch 1, ★ skip next sc, 3 sc in next sc, ch 1, sc in next ch-1 sp, ch 1, sc in next 2 ch-1 sps, ch 1, sc in next ch-1 sp, ch 1; repeat from ★ across to last 2 sc, skip next sc, 2 sc in last sc; do **not** finish off.

**Row 78:** Ch 1, turn; 2 sc in first sc, ch 1, sc in next ch-1 sp, ch 1, sc in next 2 ch-1 sps, ch 1, sc in next ch-1 sp, ch 1, ★ skip next sc, 3 sc in next sc, ch 1, sc in next ch-1 sp, ch 1, sc in next 2 ch-1 sps, ch 1, sc in next ch-1 sp, ch 1; repeat from ★ across to last 2 sc, skip next sc, 2 sc in last sc; finish off.

**Rows 79 and 80:** With Pink, repeat Rows 75 and 76.

**Rows 81 and 82:** Repeat Rows 77 and 78.

**Rows 83 and 84:** With Yellow, repeat Rows 75 and 76.

**Rows 85 and 86:** Repeat Rows 77 and 78.

**Rows 87 and 88:** With Blue, repeat Rows 75 and 76.

**Rows 89 and 90:** Repeat Rows 77 and 78.

**Rows 91 and 92:** With Orange, repeat Rows 75 and 76.

**Rows 93 and 94:** Repeat Rows 77 and 78.

**Row 95:** With **right** side facing, join Green with sc in first sc; sc in same st, ch 1, sc in next ch-1 sp, ch 1, sc in next 2 ch-1 sps, ch 1, sc in next ch-1 sp, ch 1, ★ skip next sc, 3 sc in next sc, ch 1, sc in next ch-1 sp, ch 1, sc in next 2 ch-1 sps, ch 1, sc in next ch-1 sp, ch 1; repeat from ★ across to last 2 sc, skip next sc, 2 sc in last sc; finish off.

**Row 96:** With **wrong** side facing, join White with sc in first sc; sc in same st, ch 1, sc in next ch-1 sp, ch 1, sc in next 2 ch-1 sps, ch 1, sc in next ch-1 sp, ch 1, ★ skip next sc, 3 sc in next sc, ch 1, sc in next ch-1 sp, ch 1, sc in next 2 ch-1 sps, ch 1, sc in next ch-1 sp, ch 1; repeat from ★ across to last 2 sc, skip next sc, 2 sc in last sc; finish off.

**Row 97:** With Pink, repeat Row 95.

**Row 98:** Repeat Row 96.

**Row 99:** With Yellow, repeat Row 95.

**Row 100:** Repeat Row 96.

**Row 101:** With Blue, repeat Row 95.

**Row 102:** Repeat Row 96.

**Row 103:** With Orange, repeat Row 95.

**Row 104:** Repeat Row 96.

## FINISHING

Cut a piece of cardboard 3¼" (8.25 cm) square. Wind Green, Blue or Pink loosely and evenly around the cardboard until the card is filled, then cut across one end; repeat as needed.

## Fringe

Use photo as a guide for placement. Hold two strands of Pink together; fold in half. With **right** side facing and using a crochet hook, draw the folded end up through first skipped sc on Row 51 and pull the loose ends through the folded end *(Fig. A)*; draw the knot up tightly *(Fig. B)*. Repeat in remaining skipped sc on Row 51. With Green, repeat in each skipped sc on Row 95.

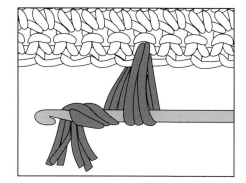

**Fig. A**

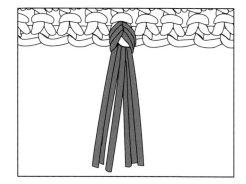

**Fig. B**

Hold two strands of Blue together; fold in half. With **wrong** side facing, and using a crochet hook, draw the folded end up through ch at base of first sc on beginning ch and pull the loose ends through the folded end; draw the knot up tightly. Repeat in ch at base of each sc across. Trim fringe as desired.

**Tassel** (Make two **each** of Green, Blue, Pink, Orange, **and** Yellow) Make 3¼" (8.25 cm) tassel *(Figs. 8a & b, page 63)*, wrapping yarn around cardboard approximately 35 times. Attach 5 tassels evenly spaced across Rows 26 and 77.

With White, sew dowel to **wrong** side of top edge.

# Textured Throw

DESIGN BY JANET L. AKINS

**EASY**

**FINISHED SIZE**
56" x 72" (142 cm x 183 cm)

**GAUGE**
In pattern,
14 sts and Rows 1-12 = 4" (10 cm)

**Gauge Swatch:** 4" (10 cm) square
With Blue, ch 15.

**Row 1:** Hdc in third ch from hook
(2 skipped chs count as first hdc) and
in each ch across: 14 hdc.

**Row 2:** Ch 1, turn; sc in each hdc
across.

**Row 3:** Ch 2 (**counts as first hdc**), turn;
hdc in next st and in each st across.

**Rows 4 and 5:** Ch 1, turn; sc in each st
across.

**Row 6:** Ch 3 (**counts as first dc**), turn;
dc in next sc and in each sc across.

**Row 7:** Repeat Row 3.

**Rows 8-12:** Repeat Rows 2-6.
Finish off.

## SHOPPING LIST

**Yarn** (Medium Weight)
[3.5 ounces, 186 yards
(100 grams, 170 meters) per skein]:

☐ Cream - 10 skeins

☐ Blue - 7 skeins

☐ Wine - 7 skeins

## Crochet Hook

☐ Size H (5 mm)

  **or** size needed for gauge

# Textured Throw

## STITCH GUIDE

**TREBLE CROCHET** *(abbreviated tr)*

YO twice, insert hook in st indicated, YO and pull up a loop (4 loops on hook), (YO and draw through 2 loops on hook) 3 times.

**DOUBLE TREBLE CROCHET** *(abbreviated dtr)*

YO 3 times, insert hook in st indicated, YO and pull up a loop (5 loops on hook), (YO and draw through 2 loops on hook) 4 times.

**LONG SINGLE CROCHET** *(abbreviated LSC)*

Working **around** previous row or rnd, insert hook in st one row or rnd **below** next st, YO and pull up a loop even with last sc made, YO and draw through both loops on hook.

- - - - - - - - - - - - - - - - - - - - - - - - - - - - - -

## BODY

With Wine, ch 182; place marker in second ch from hook for st placement.

**Row 1** (Right side)**:** Hdc in third ch from hook (**2 skipped chs count as first hdc**) and in next ch, ch 1, ★ skip next ch, hdc in next 5 chs, ch 1; repeat from ★ across to last 4 chs, skip next ch, hdc in last 3 chs: 151 hdc and 30 chs.

*Note:* Loop a short piece of yarn around any stitch to mark Row 1 as **right** side.

**Row 2:** Ch 1, turn; sc in each hdc and in each ch across changing to Blue in last sc (*Fig. 5a, page 63*): 181 sc.

**Row 3:** Ch 2 (**counts as first hdc, now and throughout**), turn; hdc in next sc, ch 3, ★ skip next 3 sc, hdc in next 3 sc, ch 3; repeat from ★ across to last 5 sc, skip next 3 sc, hdc in last 2 sc: 91 hdc and 90 chs.

**Row 4:** Ch 1, turn; sc in each hdc and in each ch across changing to Cream in last sc: 181 sc.

**Row 5:** Ch 1, turn; sc in first 2 sc, working in **front** of previous 2 rows, tr in skipped st **below** next sc, working in **front** of previous 4 rows, dtr in skipped st **below** next sc, working in **front** of previous 2 rows, skip next st from last tr made, tr in next skipped st, ★ skip next 3 sc from last sc made, sc in next sc, work LSC, sc in next sc, working in **front** of previous 2 rows, tr in skipped st **below** next sc, working in **front** of previous 4 rows, dtr in skipped st **below** next sc, working in **front** of previous 2 rows, skip next st from last tr made, tr in next skipped st; repeat from ★ across to last 5 sc, skip next 3 sc from last sc made, sc in last 2 sc.

**Row 6:** Ch 3 (**counts as first dc**), turn; dc in next sc and in each st across changing to Wine in last dc (*Fig. 5c, page 63*): 181 dc.

**Row 7:** Ch 2, turn; ★ hdc in next 5 dc, ch 1, skip next dc; repeat from ★ across to last 6 dc, hdc in last 6 dc: 152 hdc and 29 chs.

**Row 8:** Ch 1, turn; sc in each hdc and in each ch across changing to Blue in last sc: 181 sc.

**Row 9:** Ch 2, turn; hdc in next 4 sc, ch 3, ★ skip next 3 sc, hdc in next 3 sc, ch 3; repeat from ★ across to last 8 sc, skip next 3 sc, hdc in last 5 sc: 94 hdc and 87 chs.

**Row 10:** Ch 1, turn; sc in each hdc and in each ch across changing to Cream in last sc: 181 sc.

**Row 11:** Ch 1, turn; sc in first 3 sc, work LSC, sc in next sc, working in **front** of previous 2 rows, tr in skipped sc **below** next sc, working in **front** of previous 4 rows, dtr in skipped dc **below** next sc, working in **front** of previous 2 rows, skip next sc from last tr made, tr in next skipped sc, ★ skip next 3 sc from last sc made, sc in next sc, work LSC, sc in next sc, working in **front** of previous 2 rows, tr in skipped sc **below** next sc, working in **front** of previous 4 rows, dtr in skipped dc **below** next sc, working in **front** of previous 2 rows, skip next sc from last tr made, tr in next skipped sc; repeat from ★ across to last 8 sc, skip 3 sc from last sc made, sc in next sc, work LSC, sc in last 3 sc.

**Row 12:** Repeat Row 6: 181 dc.

**Row 13:** Ch 2, turn; hdc in next 2 dc, ch 1, ★ skip next dc, hdc in next 5 dc, ch 1; repeat from ★ across to last 4 dc, skip next dc, hdc in last 3 dc: 151 hdc and 30 chs.

**Rows 14-204:** Repeat Rows 2-13, 15 times; then repeat Rows 2-12 once **more**, at end of Row 204, change to Blue in last dc.

# BORDER

**Rnd 1:** Ch 1, turn; 2 sc in first dc, sc in each dc across to last dc, 3 sc in last dc; work 221 sc evenly spaced across ends of rows; working in free loops of beginning ch (*Fig. 4b, page 62*), 3 sc in first ch, sc in each ch across to marked ch, 3 sc in marked ch, remove marker, work 221 sc evenly spaced across ends of rows, sc in same st as first sc; join with slip st to first sc: 812 sc.

**Rnd 2:** Ch 2, do **not** turn; hdc in same st as joining and in each sc across to center sc of next corner 3-sc group, 3 hdc in center sc, ★ hdc in each sc across to center sc of next corner 3-sc group, 3 hdc in center sc; repeat from ★ once **more**, hdc in each sc across and in same st as first hdc; join with slip st to first hdc: 820 hdc.

**Rnd 3:** Ch 3 (**counts as first hdc plus ch 1**), hdc in same st as joining, ch 1, ★ skip next hdc, (hdc in next hdc, ch 1, skip next hdc) across to center hdc of next corner 3-hdc group, (hdc, ch 1) 3 times in center hdc; repeat from ★ 2 times **more**, skip next hdc, (hdc in next hdc, ch 1, skip next hdc) across, hdc in same st as first hdc, ch 1; join with slip st to first hdc, finish off: 418 hdc and 418 chs.

**Rnd 4:** With **right** side facing, join Wine with sc in third hdc of any corner 3-hdc group (*see Joining With Sc, page 61*); working in **front** of next ch, dc in skipped hdc one rnd **below**, ★ † sc in next hdc, working in **front** of next ch, dc in skipped hdc one rnd **below** †; repeat from † to † across to next corner 3-hdc group, (sc in next hdc, working in **front** of next ch, dc in center hdc one rnd **below**) twice; repeat from ★ around; join with slip st to first sc: 836 sts.

**Rnd 5:** Ch 2, hdc in next st and in each st around working 5 hdc in center sc of each corner 5-st group; join with slip st to first hdc, finish off: 852 hdc.

**Rnd 6:** With **right** side facing, join Cream with sc in last hdc of any corner 5-hdc group; ★ † work LSC, (sc in next hdc, work LSC) across to next corner 5-hdc group, (sc in next hdc, work LSC in corner sc one rnd **below**) twice †, sc in next hdc; repeat from ★ 2 times **more**; then repeat from † to † once; join with slip st to first sc: 852 sts.

**Rnd 7:** Ch 1, sc in same st as joining and in each st around; join with slip st to first sc, finish off.

# Vertical Wall Hanging

DESIGN BY SUE GALUCKI

 **EASY**

**FINISHED SIZE**
6¼" wide x 35" long (16 cm x 89 cm)

**GAUGE**
Each Motif = 5¾" (14.5 cm) diameter

**Gauge Swatch:** 2¾" (7 cm) diameter
Work same as First Motif through
Rnd 2, page 54: 42 dc.

## SHOPPING LIST

**Yarn** (Medium Weight)
[2.5 ounces, 120 yards
(70.9 grams, 109 meters) per skein]:

☐ White - 65 yards (59.5 meters)
☐ Navy - 30 yards (27.5 meters)
☐ Aqua - 30 yards (27.5 meters)
☐ Green - 30 yards (27.5 meters)
☐ Pink - 30 yards (27.5 meters)
☐ Rose - 30 yards (27.5 meters)

## Crochet Hook

☐ Size G (4 mm)

   **or** size needed for gauge

# Vertical Wall Hanging

## STITCH GUIDE

**SINGLE CROCHET 2 TOGETHER** *(abbreviated sc2tog)*

Insert hook in next dc on **same** Motif, YO and pull up a loop, insert hook in next dc on next Motif, YO and pull up a loop, YO and draw through all 3 loops on hook (**counts as one sc**).

**PICOT**

Ch 3, slip st in sc just made.

- - - - - - - - - - - - - - - - - - - - - - - - - - - -

Work Motifs in the following color sequences:

|  | First Motif | Second Motif | Third Motif | Fourth Motif | Fifth Motif | Sixth Motif |
|---|---|---|---|---|---|---|
| Rnd 1 | Pink | Rose | White | Aqua | Navy | Green |
| Rnd 2 | Navy | Pink | Aqua | Rose | Green | White |
| Rnd 3 | Green | Navy | Rose | Pink | White | Aqua |
| Rnd 4 | White | Green | Pink | Navy | Aqua | Rose |
| Rnd 5 | Aqua | White | Navy | Green | Rose | Pink |
| Rnd 6 | Rose | Aqua | Green | White | Pink | Navy |

## FIRST MOTIF

With first color, ch 7; join with slip st to form a ring.

**Rnd 1** (Right side)**:** Ch 5 (**counts as first dc plus ch 2, now and throughout**), (dc in ring, ch 2) 13 times; join with slip st to first dc changing to next color (**Fig. 5d, page 63**): 14 dc and 14 ch-2 sps.

*Note:* Loop a short piece of yarn around any stitch to mark Rnd 1 as **right** side.

**Rnd 2:** Ch 3 (**counts as first dc, now and throughout**), 2 dc in next ch-2 sp, (dc in next dc, 2 dc in next ch-2 sp) around; join with slip st to first dc changing to next color: 42 dc.

**Rnd 3:** Ch 1, sc in sp **before** joining (*Fig. 6, page 63*), ★ ch 3, skip next 3 dc, sc in sp **before** next dc; repeat from ★ around to last 3 dc, ch 1, skip last 3 dc, hdc in first sc to form last ch-3 sp changing to next color (*Fig. 5c, page 63*): 14 ch-3 sps.

**Rnd 4:** Ch 1, 2 sc in last ch-3 sp made, (ch 3, 2 sc in next ch-3 sp) around, ch 1, hdc in first sc to form last ch-3 sp changing to next color.

**Rnd 5:** Ch 5, dc in last ch-3 sp made, ch 2, (dc, ch 2) twice in next ch-3 sp and in each ch-3 sp around; join with slip st to first dc changing to next color: 28 ch-2 sps.

**Rnd 6:** Slip st in next ch-2 sp, ch 6 (**counts as first dc plus ch 3, now and throughout**), (dc in next ch-2 sp, ch 3) around; join with slip st to first dc, finish off.

## SECOND MOTIF

The method used to connect the Motifs is a no-sew joining also known as "join-as-you-go". After the first Motif is made, each remaining Motif is worked to the last round, then crocheted together as the last round is worked. Holding pieces with **wrong** sides together, slip st in space as indicated.

Work same as First Motif through Rnd 5: 28 ch-2 sps.

**Rnd 6** (Joining Rnd)**:** Slip st in next ch-2 sp, ch 6, dc in next ch-2 sp, (ch 3, dc in next ch-2 sp) 24 times, ch 1, with **wrong** sides together, slip st in any ch-3 sp on **previous** Motif, ch 1, ★ dc in next ch-2 sp on **new** Motif, ch 1, slip st in next ch-3 sp on **previous** Motif, ch 1; repeat from ★ once **more**; join with slip st to first dc, finish off.

## THIRD THRU SIXTH MOTIFS

Work same as First Motif through Rnd 5: 28 ch-2 sps.

**Rnd 6** (Joining rnd)**:** Slip st in next ch-2 sp, ch 6, dc in next ch-2 sp, (ch 3, dc in next ch-2 sp) 24 times, ch 1, with **wrong** sides together, skip next 11 ch-3 sps from previous joining and slip st in next ch-3 sp on **previous Motif**, ch 1, ★ dc in next ch-2 sp on **new Motif**, ch 1, slip st in next ch-3 sp on **previous Motif**, ch 1; repeat from ★ once **more**; join with slip st to first dc, finish off.

## EDGING

With **right** side facing, join White with sc in first unworked ch-2 sp on First Motif after joining *(see Joining With Sc, page 61)*; sc in same sp, † sc in next dc, work Picot, 2 sc in next ch-2 sp, (sc in next dc, work Picot, 2 sc in next ch-2 sp) 23 times, sc2tog, ★ 2 sc in next ch-2 sp, (sc in next dc, work Picot, 2 sc in next ch-2 sp) 10 times, sc2tog; repeat from ★ 3 times **more** †, 2 sc in next ch-2 sp, repeat from † to † once; join with slip st to first sc, finish off.

55

# Triangular Wrap

DESIGN BY MELISSA LEAPMAN

◼◼◻◻ **EASY**

**FINISHED SIZE**

67" wide (across top edge) x 22¾" deep (170 cm x 58 cm)

**GAUGE**

In pattern, (2 dc, ch 1, 2 dc) 4 times and 7 rows = 4" (10 cm)

**Gauge Swatch:** 7½" long x 3" high (19 cm x 7.5 cm)

Work same as Body Rows 1-5, page 58: 11 sps.

## SHOPPING LIST

**Yarn** (Light Weight)

[6 ounces, 315 yards (170 grams, 288 meters) per skein]:

☐ Blue - 1 skein

☐ Pink - 180 yards (164.5 meters)

☐ Light Pink - 110 yards (100.5 meters)

☐ Orange - 60 yards (55 meters)

☐ Aqua - 30 yards (27.5 meters)

## Crochet Hook

☐ Size I (5.5 mm)

or size needed for gauge

# Triangular Wrap

## STITCH GUIDE

### TREBLE CROCHET (abbreviated tr)
YO twice, insert hook in sp indicated, YO and pull a loop (4 loops on hook), (YO and draw through 2 loops on hook) 3 times.

### CLUSTER (uses one sp)
★ YO, insert hook in sp indicated, YO and pull up a loop, YO and draw through 2 loops on hook; repeat from ★ 2 times **more**, YO and draw through all 4 loops on hook.

### PICOT
Ch 3, slip st in third ch from hook.

- - - - - - - - - - - - - - - - - - - - - - - - -

### COLOR SEQUENCE
One row **each** of Light Pink **(Fig. 5c, page 63)**, Pink, Light Pink, 3 rows **each** of Blue, Aqua, Blue, one row of Orange, 5 rows of Blue, one row **each** of Light Pink, Pink, Light Pink, 3 rows of Blue, 2 rows of Pink, one row of Aqua, 5 rows of Blue, one row **each** of Orange, Light Pink, Orange, Light Pink, Orange, 3 rows of Pink.

- - - - - - - - - - - - - - - - - - - - - - - - -

## BODY

**Row 1:** With first color and beginning at top edge, use an adjustable loop to form a ring **(Figs. 1a-d, page 62)**, ch 5 **(counts as first tr plus ch 1, now and throughout)**, work (Cluster, ch 3, Cluster, ch 1, tr) in ring: 3 sps.

**Row 2** (Right side)**:** Ch 5, turn; (2 dc, ch 1, 2 dc) in next ch-1 sp, (sc, ch 4, sc) in next ch-3 sp, (2 dc, ch 1) twice in last ch-1 sp, tr in same sp, leave last tr unworked **(now and throughout)**: 5 sps.

**Row 3:** Ch 5, turn; (sc in next ch-1 sp, ch 4) twice, work (Cluster, ch 3, Cluster) in next ch-4 sp (corner made), ch 4, sc in next ch-1 sp, ch 4, (sc, ch 1, tr) in last ch-1 sp: 7 sps.

**Row 4:** Ch 5, turn; (2 dc, ch 1, 2 dc) in next ch-1 sp, (2 dc, ch 1, 2 dc) in each ch-4 sp across to next corner ch-3 sp, (sc, ch 4, sc) in corner ch-3 sp, (2 dc, ch 1, 2 dc) in each ch-4 sp across to last ch-1 sp, (2 dc, ch 1) twice in last ch-1 sp, tr in same sp: 9 sps.

**Row 5:** Ch 5, turn; (sc in next ch-1 sp, ch 4) across to next corner ch-4 sp, work (Cluster, ch 3, Cluster) in corner ch-4 sp, ch 4, (sc in next ch-1 sp, ch 4) across to last ch-1 sp, (sc, ch 1, tr) in last ch-1 sp: 11 sps.

**Rows 6-36:** Repeat Rows 4 and 5, 15 times; then repeat Row 4 once **more**: 73 sps.

**Row 37:** Ch 5, turn; (sc in next ch-1 sp, ch 4) across to next corner ch-4 sp, work (Cluster, ch 3, Cluster) in corner ch-4 sp, ch 4, (sc in next ch-1 sp, ch 4) across to last ch-1 sp, (sc, ch 1, tr) in last ch-1 sp: 75 sps.

**Row 38:** Ch 5, turn; dc in next ch-1 sp, (ch 1, dc in same sp) 4 times, ★ sc in next ch-4 sp, dc in next ch-4 sp, (ch 1, dc in same sp) 4 times; repeat from ★ across to next corner ch-3 sp, (sc, ch 4, sc) in corner ch-3 sp, † dc in next ch-4 sp, (ch 1, dc in same sp) 4 times, sc in next ch-4 sp †; repeat from † to † across to last ch-1 sp, (dc in last ch-1 sp, ch 1) 5 times, tr in same sp: 230 sts and 155 sps.

**Row 39:** Ch 5, turn; sc in next ch-1 sp, skip next 2 dc, dc in next dc, (ch 1, dc in same st) 4 times, ★ † sc in next sc, skip next 2 dc, dc in next dc, (ch 1, dc in same st) 4 times †; repeat from ★ across to next corner ch-4 sp, work Cluster in corner ch-4 sp, (ch 3, work Cluster in same sp) twice, skip next 2 dc, dc in next dc, (ch 1, dc in same st) 4 times, repeat from † to † across to last ch-1 sp, (sc, ch 1, tr) in last ch-1 sp.

**Row 40:** Ch 7, turn; slip st in third ch from hook, dc in next ch-1 sp, ch 1, (dc in same sp, ch 1) twice, working **around** Row 39, sc in ch-1 sp **below** next sc, ch 1, skip next 2 dc, dc in next dc, (ch 1, dc in same dc) twice, work Picot, (dc in same dc, ch 1) 3 times, † working **around** last 2 rows, 2 sc in ch-4 sp 3 rows **below**, ch 1, skip next 2 dc, dc in next dc, (ch 1, dc in same dc) twice, work Picot, (dc in same dc, ch 1) 3 times †; repeat from † to † across to corner 3-Cluster group, 2 sc in next ch-3 sp, ch 1, dc in next Cluster, (ch 1, dc in same st) twice, work Picot, (dc in same st, ch 1) 3 times, 2 sc in next ch-3 sp, ch 1, skip next 2 dc, dc in next dc, (ch 1, dc in same dc) twice, work Picot, (dc in same dc, ch 1) 3 times, repeat from † to † across to last sc, working **around** Row 39, sc in ch-1 sp **below** last sc, (ch 1, dc in last ch-1 sp) 3 times, work Picot, ch 1, tr in same sp; finish off.

# General Instructions

## ABBREVIATIONS

| | |
|---|---|
| ch(s) | chain(s) |
| cm | centimeters |
| dc | double crochet(s) |
| dtr | double treble crochet(s) |
| hdc | half double crochet(s) |
| LSC | Long Single Crochet(s) |
| mm | millimeters |
| Rnd(s) | Round(s) |
| sc | single crochet(s) |
| sc2tog | single crochet 2 together |
| sp(s) | space(s) |
| st(s) | stitch(es) |
| tr | treble crochet(s) |
| YO | yarn over |

## SYMBOLS & TERMS

★ — work instructions following ★ as many **more** times as indicated in addition to the first time.

† to † — work all instructions from first † to second † **as many** times as specified.

( ) or [ ] — work enclosed instructions **as many** times as specified by the number immediately following **or** work all enclosed instructions in the stitch or space indicated **or** contains explanatory remarks.

colon (:) — the number(s) given after a colon at the end of a row or round denote(s) the number of stitches or spaces you should have on that row or round.

## GAUGE

Exact gauge is **essential** for proper size. Before beginning your project, make the sample swatch given in the individual instructions in the yarn and hook specified. After completing the swatch, measure it, counting your stitches and rows or rounds carefully. If your swatch is larger or smaller than specified, **make another, changing hook size to get the correct gauge**. Keep trying until you find the size hook that will give you the specified gauge.

## MARKERS

Markers are used to help distinguish the beginning of each round being worked. Place a 2" (5 cm) scrap piece of yarn before the first stitch of each round, moving marker after each round is complete.

## JOINING WITH SC

When instructed to join with sc, begin with a slip knot on hook. Insert hook in stitch or space indicated, YO and pull up a loop, YO and draw through both loops on hook.

## JOINING WITH HDC

When instructed to join with hdc, begin with a slip knot on hook. YO, holding loop on hook, insert hook in stitch or space indicated, YO and pull up a loop, YO and draw through all 3 loops on hook.

## JOINING WITH DC

When instructed to join with dc, begin with a slip knot on hook. YO, holding loop on hook, insert hook in stitch or space indicated, YO and pull up a loop (3 loops on hook), (YO and draw through 2 loops on hook) twice.

## JOINING WITH TR

When instructed to join with tr, begin with a slip knot on hook. YO twice, holding loops on hook, insert hook in stitch or space indicated, YO and pull up a loop (4 loops on hook), (YO and draw through 2 loops on hook) 3 times.

## CROCHET TERMINOLOGY

| United States | | International |
|---|---|---|
| slip stitch (slip st) | = | single crochet (sc) |
| single crochet (sc) | = | double crochet (dc) |
| half double crochet (hdc) | = | half treble crochet (htr) |
| double crochet (dc) | = | treble crochet (tr) |
| treble crochet (tr) | = | double treble crochet (dtr) |
| double treble crochet (dtr) | = | triple treble crochet (ttr) |
| triple treble crochet (tr tr) | = | quadruple treble crochet (qtr) |
| skip | = | miss |

## CROCHET HOOKS

| United States | Metric (mm) | United States | Metric (mm) | United States | Metric (mm) |
|---|---|---|---|---|---|
| B-1 | 2.25 | 7 | 4.5 | M/N-13 | 9 |
| C-2 | 2.75 | H-8 | 5 | N/P-15 | 10 |
| D-3 | 3.25 | I-9 | 5.5 | P/Q | 15 |
| E-4 | 3.5 | J-10 | 6 | Q | 16 |
| F-5 | 3.75 | K-10½ | 6.5 | S | 19 |
| G-6 | 4 | L-11 | 8 | | |

| | | |
|---|---|---|
| ▮▯▯▯ BEGINNER | | Projects for first-time crocheters using basic stitches. Minimal shaping. |
| ▮▮▯▯ EASY | | Projects using yarn with basic stitches, repetitive stitch patterns, simple color changes, and simple shaping and finishing. |
| ▮▮▮▯ INTERMEDIATE | | Projects using a variety of techniques, such as basic lace patterns or color patterns, mid-level shaping and finishing. |
| ▮▮▮▮ EXPERIENCED | | Projects with intricate stitch patterns, techniques and dimension, such as non-repeating patterns, multi-color techniques, fine threads, small hooks, detailed shaping and refined finishing. |

| Yarn Weight Symbol & Names | LACE 0 | SUPER FINE 1 | FINE 2 | LIGHT 3 | MEDIUM 4 | BULKY 5 | SUPER BULKY 6 | JUMBO 7 |
|---|---|---|---|---|---|---|---|---|
| Type of Yarns in Category | Fingering, size 10 crochet thread | Sock, Fingering, Baby | Sport, Baby | DK, Light Worsted | Worsted, Afghan, Aran | Chunky, Craft, Rug | Super Bulky, Roving | Jumbo, Roving |
| Crochet Gauge* Ranges in Single Crochet to 4" (10 cm) | 32-42 sts** | 21-32 sts | 16-20 sts | 12-17 sts | 11-14 sts | 8-11 sts | 6-9 sts | 5 sts and fewer |
| Advised Hook Size Range | Steel*** 6 to 8, Regular hook B-1 | B-1 to E-4 | E-4 to 7 | 7 to I-9 | I-9 to K-10½ | K-10½ to M/N-13 | M/N-13 to Q | Q and larger |

*GUIDELINES ONLY: The chart above reflects the most commonly used gauges and hook sizes for specific yarn categories.

** Lace weight yarns are usually crocheted with larger hooks to create lacy openwork patterns. Accordingly, a gauge range is difficult to determine. Always follow the gauge stated in your pattern.

*** Steel crochet hooks are sized differently from regular hooks–the higher the number, the smaller the hook, which is the reverse of regular hook sizing.

## ADJUSTABLE LOOP

Wind yarn around two fingers to form a ring *(Fig. 1a)*. Slide yarn off fingers and grasp the strands at the top of the ring *(Fig. 1b)*. Insert hook from **front** to **back** into the ring, pull up a loop, YO and draw through loop on hook to lock ring *(Fig. 1c)* (st made does **not** count as part of beginning ch of first rnd). Working around **both** strands, follow instructions to work sts in the ring, then pull yarn tail to close *(Fig. 1d)*.

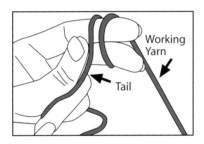

**Fig. 1a**

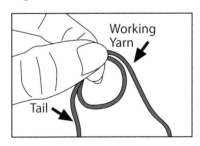

**Fig. 1b**

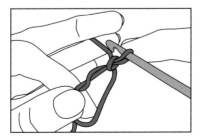

**Fig. 1c**

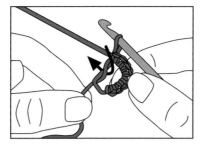

**Fig. 1d**

## BACK RIDGE

Work only in loops indicated by arrows *(Fig. 2)*.

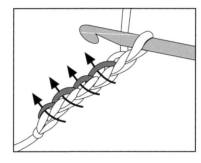

**Fig. 2**

## BACK OR FRONT LOOPS ONLY

Work only in loop(s) indicated by arrow *(Fig. 3)*.

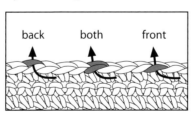

**Fig. 3**

## FREE LOOPS

After working in Back or Front Loops Only on a row or round, there will be a ridge of unused loops. These are called the free loops. Later, when instructed to work in the free loops of the same row or round, work in these loops *(Fig. 4a)*. When instructed to work in free loops of a chain, work in loop indicated by arrow *(Fig. 4b)*.

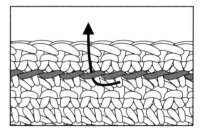

**Fig. 4a**

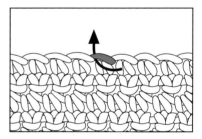

**Fig. 4b**

# CHANGING COLORS

To change colors while **working a stitch,** work the last stitch to within one step of completion, drop yarn, hook new yarn *(Fig. 5a, b, or c)* and draw through all loops on hook. Do **not** cut yarn until indicated.

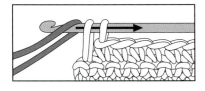

**Fig. 5a**

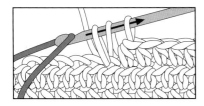

**Fig. 5b**

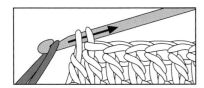

**Fig. 5c**

To change colors while **joining with a slip st**, drop yarn, insert hook in first stitch, hook new yarn and draw through st and loop on hook *(Fig. 5d)*; cut old color unless otherwise instructed.

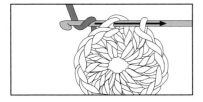

**Fig. 5d**

# WORKING IN A SPACE BEFORE A STITCH

When instructed to work in a space **before** a stitch or in space **between** stitches, insert hook in space indicated by arrow *(Fig. 6)*.

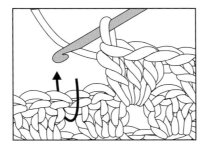

**Fig. 6**

# WORKING AROUND A STITCH

Work in stitch or space indicated, inserting hook in direction of arrow *(Fig. 7)*.

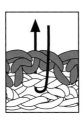

**Fig. 7**

# TASSEL

Cut a piece of cardboard 3" (7.5 cm) wide and as long as you want your finished tassel to be. Wind a double strand of yarn around the cardboard. Cut an 18" (45.5 cm) length of yarn and insert it under all of the strands at the top of the cardboard; pull up **tightly** and tie securely. Leave the yarn ends long enough to attach the tassel. Cut the yarn at the opposite end of the cardboard and then remove it *(Fig. 8a)*. Cut a 18" (15 cm) length of yarn and wrap it **tightly** around the tassel several times, ½" (12 mm) below the top *(Fig. 8b)*; tie securely. Trim the ends.

**Fig. 8a**

**Fig. 8b**

# Yarn Information

The items in this book were made using a variety of yarns. Any brand of the specific weight of yarn may be used. It is best to refer to the yardage/meters when determining how many balls or skeins to purchase. Remember, to achieve the same look, it is the weight of yarn that is important, not the brand of yarn.

For your convenience, listed below are the specific yarns used to create our photography models. Because yarn manufacturers make frequent changes to their product lines, you may sometimes find it necessary to use a substitute yarn or to search for the discontinued product at alternate suppliers (locally or online).

## STRIPED BASKET
*Lily® Sugar'n Cream®*
Yellow - #00073 Sunshine
Pink - #01740 Hot Pink
White - 00001 White

## BRIGHT COASTER SET
*Lily® Sugar'n Cream®*
Yellow - #00010 Yellow
Pink - #01740 Hot Pink
Orange - #01628 Hot Orange
Green - #01712 Hot Green

## WAVY COWL
*Bernat® Super Value™*
White - #07391 White
Blue - #00616 Peacock
Green - #53223 Grass
Purple - #53333 Mulberry
Pink - #53417 Peony Pink
Yellow - #00608 Bright Yellow

## FLOWER MUG COZY
*Red Heart® Super Saver®*
White - #311 White
Pink - #718 Shocking Pink
Green - #368 Paddy Green

## FLORAL MARKETBAG
*Premier® Yarns Cotton Fair™*
Main Color - #27-01 White
**Contrasting Colors**
Blue - #27-04 Turquoise
Purple - #27-09 Lavender
Peach - #27-07 Bright Peach
Green - #27-10 Leaf Green

## VIBRANT MANDALA
*Caron® Simply Soft®*
White - #9701 White
Blue - #9767 Royal Blue
Aqua - #9708 Robins Egg
Pink - #9775 Neon Pink
Orange - #9774 Neon Orange

## DAISIES NOTEBOOK COVER
*Lion Brand® Mandala®*
Main Color - #209 Gnome
*Caron® Simply Soft®*
White - #9701 White
Yellow - #9612 Super Duper Yellow
Green - #9607 Limelight

## OVAL RUG
*Lion Brand® Hometown USA®*
Blue - #105 Detroit Blue
Red - #113 Cincinnati Red
Yellow - #158 Pittsburgh Yellow
Purple - #147 Minneapolis Purple
Green - #171 Key Lime

## TASSELED PILLOW
*Red Heart® Baby Hugs™ Light*
White - #3001 Frosting
Green - #3625 Sprout
Pink - #3740 Happy
Blue - #3820 Sky
Purple - #3538 Lilac

## RIPPLE WALL HANGING
*Caron® Simply Soft®*
White - #9701 White
Green - #9607 Limelight
Blue - #9784 Cobalt Blue
Pink - #9604 Watermelon
Orange - #9605 Mango
Yellow - #9612 Super Duper Yellow

## TEXTURED THROW
*Red Heart® Chic Sheep by Marly Bird™*
Cream - #5311 Lace
Blue - #5693 Poolside
Wine - #5907 Sangria

## VERTICAL WALL HANGING
*Lion Brand® 24/7 Cotton®*
White - #100 White
Navy - #110 Navy
Aqua - #102 Aqua
Green - #172 Grass
Pink - #101 Pink
Rose - #142 Rose

## TRIANGULAR WRAP
*Caron® Simply Soft®*
Blue - #9784 Cobalt Blue
Pink - #9804 Watermelon
Light Pink - #9719 Soft Pink
Orange - #9605 Mango
Aqua - #9708 Robins Egg

We have made every effort to ensure that these instructions are accurate and complete. We cannot, however, be responsible for human error, typographical mistakes, or variations in individual work.

Items made and instructions tested by Belinda Baxter, Dena Casey, Kimberly Holloway, Amanda Loggins, and Barbara Schou.

Production Team: Instructional/Technical Editor - Lois J. Long; Senior Graphic Artist - Lora Puls; Graphic Artists - Michael Douglas and Amy L. Teeter; Photo Stylist - Lori Wenger; and Photographer - Jason Masters.

Library of Congress Control Number: 2018945248

Made in U.S.A.